EXPRESSION

In
Music

VanderCook

HAL•LEONARD®

L-249

FOREWORD

$\mathcal{D}$EFINITE and specific instructions on the playing of music with expression are always needed, and such information should be sought after continually by every serious-minded player as well as by every teacher and director.

Throughout the country, there are thousands of musical organizations whose members are quite capable of playing or singing every note on the printed page before them. Interest and enthusiasm in such organizations, however, can only be maintained when they show steady improvement at both rehearsals and public appearances. When a group has been drilled by an instructor who has an experienced understanding of the grammar of music and the factors governing playing with expression, it is readily discernible that the players are attempting to meet the teacher's ideals; that they are striving in every possible way to secure pleasing results and to do something besides merely sounding all the notes.

The importance of playing in good style with proper expression is too often neglected by the teacher and, as a natural consequence, by those studying under him. The student who understands and utilizes the rules for playing in good style readily learns to increase his endurance and to execute passages in music that would be quite impossible to master without this necessary knowledge. He really learns to rest while he is playing. The authority Arban, in referring to playing with expression, writes: "This circumstance (accent and expression) affords the performer an opportunity to rest while he continues to play and enables him to introduce effective contrasts into the execution at the same time. By little artifices of this kind and by skillfully husbanding his resources, the player will reach the end of the most fatiguing piece without difficulty and with a reserve of strength and power which, when brought to bear on the final measures of a performance, never fails to produce its effect on an audience."

Rapid advancement in both sight reading and interpretation is possible for the student if he will study the basic concepts of musical expression that enable a performer to play in good style. The musician who underestimates the importance of the subject is overlooking one of the most important factors leading to ultimate success. The teacher who has not given much thought before this to the points discussed will be pleased and surprised at the results he will secure in the training of his students and musical organizations if he follows closely the suggestions offered in the succeeding pages.

In the beginning, the teacher should drill the students on the simplest musical figures one at a time, then gradually introduce and explain new figures, always bearing in mind the necessity of a general review of everything previously introduced and practiced.

H. A. VanderCook

TABLE OF CONTENTS

CHAPTER ONE

A WELL-KNOWN soloist who traveled extensively with some of the great concert bands of his day once said: "It is truly amazing to note the larger number of marvelous performers on the different instruments throughout the country. Hundreds of them have visited me and played for me. The vast amount of execution, wonderful register, lip trills, etc., that many of them displayed is remarkable. However, so many of them seem to be restricted to just these points. They seem utterly devoid of the main requisite, expression or style."

The schooled musician will instantly recognize the truth of this statement. The beginner seldom realizes it until he attempts to play a passage after hearing an artist interpret it. Then, and only then, he feels that while he may play all the notes, there is something important lacking. After that, if he develops a desire to do something besides get all the notes, he has started on the right road towards playing with expression, for, as the wise old Bandmaster once said, "It is not what you play, it's the way you play it." The full meaning of this sentence should always be borne in mind by the aspiring student.

At best, a page of music may be considered as a blue print of the plans and specifications of the melody and the manner in which it is to be played. The length of each note is given and its register is indicated; the passage may be marked *forte* or *piano*, as the case may be, and the *tempo* is usually clearly indicated. However, even if he follows these plainly marked directions to the letter, the performer will still find a great deal lacking in his rendition of the passage, especially so after he has heard an experienced and artistic musician interpret it.

There are certain principles that govern good style and make expression. Many of them cannot be reduced to letters or figures on

1

the printed page as they would leave little space for the notes and standard markings and would seriously affect the general legibility.

Admitting that the *tempo* (the speed at which a passage should be played) is of importance in the rendition of a melody, there still remains a greater point in imparting expression to a musical composition. This essential element is correct accent, or emphasis. After good tone and proper *tempo*, correct accent is the factor that is necessary for expression in music.

One of the mistakes generally committed by the beginner is that of playing in a monotone; a sort of humdrum, hand-organ style. Even if the performer discovers this fault in his playing, usually he is at a loss as to how to remedy the defect. In all probability he lacks the necessary knowledge that governs correct emphasis and accent. While it is not intended that the principles laid down in this book should be applied in every instance, they will be of great assistance in most cases and will have a tendency to improve the playing of anyone in need of them.

"Anyone can play loudly, but it takes a musician to play softly" is another well-known saying that can be applied truthfully to any music student, but especially those on a brass instrument. To gain any experience and derive any benefit from the following chapters, brass students must be able to play softly.

Frequently, many who claim that they can do this are amazed, when they are put to the test, to find that their best efforts will result in a windy, wheezy tone, or that the tone will stop altogether. Any brass instrument player who has not already made use of the examples in Dr. Herbert L. Clarke's wonderful book, "Technical Studies, Second Series," will feel encouraged and inspired at the beneficial results that careful practice of these studies will bring. He will soon be able to play as softly as a flute or muted violin.

Likewise, those playing stringed instruments must be able to draw a smooth, steady bow, which will result in the production of a tone of richness and purity.

Many players (both beginners and more experienced musicians) assume that all the notes in a passage marked *ff* should be played extremely *forte*. This is as serious an error as the supposition that all the notes in a passage marked *pp* should be played very softly. Accents in a melody should be as natural and indiscernible as those in ordinary conversation.

To illustrate the importance of accent and emphasis take the following sentence of only five words. Read it five times, placing marked accent on the first word the first time and speaking all the remaining words softly. The second time, put the accent on the second word, etc. In reading each line, place the emphasis on the word in capital letters.

WERE you there that night?
Were YOU there that night?
Were you THERE that night?
Were you there THAT night?
Were you there that NIGHT?

You will notice during this experiment that each time you changed the accent you gave the sentence a different meaning. Similarly, if a performer accents the wrong notes, he gives the music an interpretation never intended by the composer. To play with expression, some notes must be emphasized in even the softest passage, while to play a *forte* passage well, some of the notes should be played softer in relation to the others.

Unfortunately, the average young instrumentalist's sole ambition is to play as loudly as he can and to squeeze out as high a tone as possible. This deplorable condition is often due to the fact that he has not been taught to play in good style. Many of our finished performers will remember that they were told that experience was the sole factor needed to make them play in good style, or that they would have to just "pick it up." The fact of the matter is that for the first few years they heard little but very bad style, and, consequently, had a hard time acquiring good style after many bad habits were formed.

The following chapters contain many printed examples of music with the correct accents marked so clearly that they can be understood without difficulty. The study of this system will soon develop a practical understanding of the principles of accent and their application to a melody or musical composition.

CHAPTER TWO

*W*ITH all of the high-sounding titles that may be given to it, and no matter how poetically it may be described, expression in music consists of well-placed and intelligent accent or emphasis. Experienced musicians who readily recognize this fact give it the rough and ready name of "playing in good style," and next to good tone, consider it their most valuable stock in trade. "He has good temperament" or "he has good style" goes a long way in describing the ability of a fellow artist. Many able performers play with good expression by listening repeatedly to experienced players and noting their method of interpretation. This is an excellent procedure for those who have the opportunity.

"He played from the soul" or "he put his heart into the music" is another way of saying that the performer placed emphasis and accent on certain notes in an intelligent and grammatical manner and that he shaded others with practiced care.

The musician who is accustomed to playing by merely getting all the notes will find that it requires something besides learning the rules of good style if he is to show marked improvement in his playing. It takes practice, practice and more practice, but the results justify the time and effort spent. Remember what David Starr Jordan said? "Only that becomes real and helpful to any man which has cost the sweat of his brow, the effort of his brain, or the anguish of his soul." Little advancement towards perfection can be made without concentration, practice and repeated attempts.

Admittedly, the most difficult task all music teachers find themselves confronted with is that of teaching pupils the principles of playing in good style. While it may be comparatively easy for the teacher to explain this subject in a few words, invariably the pupil will find it difficult to grasp the meaning of the explanation and apply it. When the pupil is asked to place especial stress, emphasis or accent on some particular note, he immediately plays all the surrounding notes *forte!* When asked to play the surrounding notes softly, he will play the long, dotted or accented notes *piano*. At this point, if he is at all observing, the student will find that he lacks control of his breath, or in the case of string players, control of his bow. He will discover that he can play loudly all the time quite easily, that he plays with an inferior tonal quality when he attempts to reduce the volume of tone, and that it is quite impossible for him to play one *forte* tone followed by two *piano* tones or vice versa. This is entirely due to the fact that he has never practiced playing softly.

Instead of discouraging the pupil, this defect should be the means of pointing his way toward success. He has discovered his greatest impediment in playing with expression and he should go to work immediately to overcome this difficulty. As soon as the student has gained some degree of control, an immediate change for the better will result. Without this attainment, no progress can be made toward the art of playing with expression.

Since it is a well-known fact that listening to the interpretations of fine experienced musicians is one of the best ways to improve a player's style of performance, it is strange that so few wind and string players take advantage of two readily accessible opportunities to study the masters in their field—the radio and the phonograph. Many fine bands, orchestras, and soloists, as well as some ensemble groups, broadcast regularly. A systematically careful, critical listening will bring many examples of brilliant technic, correct intonation and well placed emphasis to the student. It will repay the serious player many times over to follow radio program listings until he is familiar with all the opportunities to hear these masters that our radio stations offer, and then let no distraction interfere with a close study of the interpretations as rendered by the finest talent available.

The phonograph also offers many opportunities to the ambitious player. There are innumerable really fine instrumental and vocal recordings available. They can be played again and again so that the student can analyze and study difficult and interesting passages which require close attention and can gain from them a correct understanding of what is meant by emphasis, shading, phrasing, *crescendo* and *diminuendo,* as well as the greatest phase in solo playing—*tempo rubato.*

All too often a director will listen to a masterly recording of a fine composition, obtain a copy of the same number for his organization, and, through carelessness or disregard of correct emphasis, allow it to be performed in such a manner that it is scarcely recognizable. The exact opposite effect might have been obtained if the leader had been careful to imitate all of the fine points of the recording. As mentioned before, the development of good style can be largely based on analyzing the performances of those who are recognized as artists. As the vast majority of students are not in a position to associate or study with these artists, those who desire to attain a fine degree of perfection in their interpretations will find this an excellent, worth while procedure.

Frequently the question arises as to just what the artist did to make his rendition so pleasing and effective. The ability to play all the notes, cover the entire register of the instrument and perform at the same rate of speed that the artist used who made the recording, although important, will not necessarily guarantee similar results. Factors contributing to ineffective performance are numerous; one or more of the following common mistakes may be involved:

Too much monotone—all the notes are too near the same volume.

Long notes are too soft as compared with the shorter ones and short notes are too loud in comparison with the longer ones.

Long tones are allowed to diminish in volume before their time value has expired. Exceptions are sometimes found when long tones are otherwise marked.

Short notes are almost invariably too loud for the long notes that accompany them, especially in a run or an arpeggio of sixteenths.

Too much time is consumed by wind instrument players in taking a breath especially in *andante* passages, or, not enough air is inhaled when breath is taken.

Those playing stringed instruments often run out of bow; this is due from either attempting to play too many notes in the same bow, or from not being able to control the bow sufficiently well to use it in its entirety.

All dotted notes are curtailed making them *staccato;* that is, shorter than they are written. This is one of the most glaring faults of many student musicians.

The note following a dotted note is played with the same volume that was given to the dotted note. (Read that sentence over four or five times. It is important to understand it fully.)

It is a fact that nearly all inexperienced players commit the same errors that detract from good style and expression. It is also true that all good performers avoid these well-known errors. It requires no great physical effort to play in good style; in fact, it is usually easier to play well than to play incorrectly. The player who does not practice the art of shading and emphasis is over-working his muscles and breathing to the limit at all times; therefore, he cannot take advantage of the passages which would allow him to ease up in his efforts while still playing.

As preparation to studying the application of the well-known principles of musical expression, the student should practice playing very softly. No one can play with expression until he is able to govern the tone to the extent that it will sound as softly as the flute is played.

Remember to hold the instrument, head and body very quietly while practicing softly as the tone will often stop at the least movement. From this point on, no more time or effort should be wasted on playing loudly or attempting to reach high notes. That phase of musicianship can be put aside while learning to play with expression. As much spare time as possible should be put into the practice of playing softly so that it will become easy and natural to produce sweet pure tones without effort.

CHAPTER THREE

*I*N music, we often meet a figure that is composed of a dotted eighth note followed by a sixteenth note. Nearly as often as we find this combination, it is abused and played incorrectly. The incorrect interpretation of this figure will tend to destroy good expression in a musical phrase, no matter how carefully the balance of the notes are played.

An illustration of this figure is contained in the march tune shown in the following example.

No. 1

Close attention to the usual rendition of the above passage reveals that it is often played as if it had been written this way:

No. 2

It is a common fault to play this melody with a full measure of six-eighth time as well as one beat of six-eighth time in the third measure. When a dotted eighth note is followed by a sixteenth note, it should not sound like a triplet with the middle note omitted.

This dotted eighth note and sixteenth note figure is a very small factor; however, when it is played like a triplet several times in succession it begins to sound badly and is certainly not the effect the composer desired. It should be remembered that the time value of the dotted eighth is three times that of the sixteenth note. Furthermore, the dotted eighth note should be played with three times the power or accent that is given to the sixteenth note that follows it. This usually applies every time this figure is used in a musical composition.

The above example affords an excellent opportunity for practicing accent or expression. Remember to play softly, and in this instance, a softer note follows an accented or louder note. The phrase will have to be practiced very slowly numerous times, exaggerating the volume of the eighth note and diminishing the volume of the sixteenth note. Only long and careful practice can develop the ability to perform this figure properly at all times and at any tempo. This time and effort is well worth while, for once the performer acquires the correct interpretation, his ear will demand its use and he will instantly notice when others play it incorrectly.

Many may experience a little difficulty in understanding the following directions in connection with the dotted eighth note and sixteenth note figure. Whenever this figure appears in a passage two or more times, the breath current should stop for an instant after each dotted eighth note. In other words, each dotted eighth note should be played slightly shorter than written. The sixteenth note, however, is given its full value for it is played *legato*. When only one of these figures appears in a melody, the dotted eighth note should be played *legato* (given its full value), for in that case the dotted eighth note must sound like a quarter note followed by a light grace note. Therefore, the melody given at the beginning of this chapter should be played as if it had been written like this:

No. 3

Numerals have been placed over the notes in the above example (3, 1 and 4). They refer to the relative volume or accent that should be given to each note. The following suggestions will help to interpret this melody correctly.

In the first measure, the first as well as the second dotted eighth notes should be nearly as long as three sixteenth notes — lacking only a thirty-second beat — and that is where the tone is stopped for an instant only. On both beats in the first measures, the dotted eighth notes should receive three times the volume that is given to the following sixteenth notes. The sixteenth note in each of these beats cannot be played too softly. The chances are if the player tries to overdo the matter, he will get it just about right. The accent of the eighth notes should be exaggerated at first and long careful practice will gradually bring about good results.

In the second measure, the eighth notes receive only one point of accent and should be made as short as sixteenth notes. This is quite essential to good expression.

In the third measure, the dotted eighth note should be given its full value, because the figure occurs only once. In this case, the dotted eighth note receives the same volume as is given to a quarter note. It should receive four points of accent; in other words, it should be played four times as loudly as the following sixteenth note. Care must also be taken that the tone is not broken between the dotted eighth note and the sixteenth note in this measure. This sounds like a trivial matter, but good style depends wholly on just such small points as this.

In the fourth measure, the volume of the half note should not diminish before its time value expires. This is a general fault among careless players. The thoughtful student will swell the long notes stronger at their finish, or hold them as full and round to the end as when he began sounding them. This appears like another small matter, but the habit of diminishing the tone volume of these long notes before their time value has expired is indulged in by thousands of performers in brass, reed and string instruments as well as by numerous singers. This does not mean that a long note should not be diminished when it is so indicated, but it does mean that this manner of playing is undesirable when it makes every phrase ending with a long tone sound as if the musician had exhausted his reserve of power and needed a quick intake of breath to preserve life.

A dotted quarter note followed by an eighth note should be treated in the same manner as the figure described in the foregoing paragraphs. In No. 4, the same march melody has been written in *alla breve tempo.* In this form it should receive the same treatment as far as accent is concerned as is given to the dotted eighth note followed by a sixteenth note. Upon examination of this example, it will be seen that the figure should be played so that it will sound exactly like the first example in this chapter.

No. 4

In this case the emphasis is indicated in the same manner in which the melody was marked when it was written in 2/4 tempo.

In the next illustration, the same melody has been written in 2/4 tempo once more, but in a broader form. Writing the melody in this manner results in a *grandioso* movement; its accent should become more marked, but still in the same proportion as has been described for the dotted eighth note and sixteenth note figure. Observe that the dotted quarter note is equal to three eighth notes in time value. Also notice that a slight change has been made in the accent in the third and fourth measures as these quarter notes must receive slightly more emphasis than was given to them when they were written as eighth notes.

No. 5

To play the above melody in good style and with the proper expression, the correct value of each note must be observed. This point will be easily understood by comparing the melody in No. 5 with the original one in this chapter. No. 5 should sound as if it were written as follows:

No. 6

In the above illustration, in measure five, each note should receive its full value. If a melody is made up largely of dotted quarter notes followed by eighth notes, there should be a slight curtailment of the time value of each quarter note. However, when there is only one dotted quarter note followed by an eighth note, that dotted quarter note is usually played *legato* (sustained for its full value). While there are a few isolated instances where this procedure is not applicable, in most cases it is good taste to observe it.

Diligent and conscientious observance of the above rules will soon convince most players that absolute tone control and the ability to play softly at will are highly essential if he wishes to perform with expression.

CHAPTER FOUR

*C*OMBINATIONS of notes producing figures that are rarely used in musical compositions usually do not greatly offend the educated ear when incorrectly played as to accent and time value. Figures that are often met with, however, will soon grate and grind on the ear of the schooled musician if improperly interpreted. Often a student will play on in blissful ignorance and in a manner highly satisfactory to his own ear, not realizing that his entire interpretation is faulty.

Syncopated figures are used very extensively in many compositions of modern origin. As they are so very often interpreted incorrectly, this chapter is devoted to an explanation of the common faults, as well as to the remedies to be applied in performing syncopation. It is seldom misunderstood or incorrectly interpreted when built on simple form such as this:

No. 7

To many, the melody in the above example is quite easy to interpret at the first rendition. It is not difficult to give the proper amount of accent to all of the half notes and keep the emphasis off all of the quarter notes. It is only when syncopation is played with greater rapidity that misinterpretation results. This becomes self evident during the rendition of a syncopated passage as set forth in No. 8. In this

15

excerpt, the melody used in No. 7 has been written in a form that
requires it to be played twice as fast.

No. 8

Invariably, in playing these figures, the length of the syncopated
note is curtailed and the proportionate emphasis required for good style
is reduced. Thus this passage will sound as if it had been written in
this manner:

No. 9

Naturally, the above rendition entirely destroys the effect origi-
nally intended. By curtailing the length of the syncopated notes the
required accent is lessened and the passage becomes meaningless and
quite monotonous.

This brings us to the greatest mistake of all in the interpretation
of syncopation. If the melody were written in eighth and sixteenth
notes, so that it would have to be played still more rapidly, it should
sound as if it had been written in the following manner:

No. 10

When this passage is practiced, many will interpret it in a manner that to them sounds quite correct, but in reality sounds as if it had been written this way:

No. 11

An examination of the above reveals that the emphasis intended in the first place has been almost completely obliterated by curtailing the time value of the syncopated notes.

If the wind instrument student really wants to improve his expression in playing syncopated figures, he should guard strongly against trying to place the proper emphasis correctly by attacking too hard with his tongue. This act is certain to destroy the quality of the tone. It should always be kept in mind that an accented note, in spite of the fact that it requires a somewhat sharper attack, must have the same fine tonal quality as an unaccented note. Accented notes should be played with additional breath, not merely with an attacking stroke of the tongue. This is a good point to remember and one which should be worked on diligently during practice.

In the case of playing stringed instruments, not only should additional bow be employed when accenting a note, but also more pressure should be placed on the bow, the pressure being brought about through the thumb and first three fingers of the right hand.

To those who have given no special attention to the relative volume required for each note in a passage of music, the marked accents which have been placed over the notes in the accompanying examples may seem difficult to follow. In fact, it is easy to get the impression that to study or place correct emphasis on a phrase is an involved affair. This is not true. By practicing very slowly at first, and at the same time concentrating on the results, good expression will soon become a habit. It will be as natural to place the accent correctly as it is to judge the exact time value of each note on the printed page. Often we hear a player remark: "Just let me play the passage over a few times and I will get something out of it." It is not always possible to allow him this opportunity; at times he may be required to play a musical composition as correctly as possible at the first reading. This can be accomplished only by thorough acquaintanceship with the rules of expression so that the performer can produce any passage with a good tone and a smooth style whenever called upon to do so. He must intelligently place the emphasis exactly where it belongs. There is no such thing as "your style" or "my style." There is only one correct style which must be attained through arduous, diligent practice.

Hundreds of examples, followed by numerous explanations, could be written on the various forms of syncopation and the relative accents necessary to perform them grammatically; however, the observing and ingenious player does not need them. The principal mistakes committed in the playing of these figures are given below with the remedy for each one indicated. With these principles in mind at all times, the interpretation of syncopation is certain to improve naturally and with dispatch.

First: The notes preceding and following the syncopated note should be played somewhat shorter than written and about four times as softly as the syncopated or emphasized note.

Secondly: The syncopated note should be played nearly its full written length and should receive about four times the volume of the notes preceding and following it.

Thirdly: The syncopated note should never be played with a rough tone. When it is an eighth note, great care should be exercised so that the note is not attacked too hard in order to place the required emphasis upon it. Remember, an accented note requires additional volume.

Accent and emphasis as applied to a musical passage are difficult to define. The subject is truly a sensitive one as authorities seldom seem to agree upon it, while many of the best teachers avoid it entirely. Many performers consider it merely a question of taste. Musicians of various nationalities usually perform differently. An example of this is found in the fact that while the German and Italian musicians may place emphasis on the same notes, the latter will invariably play with more contrast, more fire and vim than the former.

The common vaudeville or theatre pit style of playing is something that no one should attempt to imitate. Neither is it in good taste to terrify an audience with a sudden outburst of tone when interpreting a musical composition. However, it must be admitted that what appears to be exceedingly heavy accent to one musician will seem quite normal to another. The main objective to be kept in mind at all times, is to avoid monotony without becoming sensational. To accomplish this, the accent must be varied, reasonable and intelligent. The study of emphasis will gradually bring about this end. The performer must know where to place the accent and must be capable of playing the unaccented notes softly. They, who at first exaggerate by making the accented notes too loud and the unaccented notes too soft, will often make the most rapid progress in the study of playing with expression.

CHAPTER FIVE

*A*NOTHER fault common to the renditions of many students is the interpretation of groups of notes that are tied or slurred. When two notes on the same degree of the staff are tied, the second note should receive almost the same volume as the first note. An illustration of such a figure is given in the following excerpt:

No. 12

However, when two notes on different degrees of the staff are slurred, the second note should receive less volume than is given to the first note. The following melody illustrates this point:

No. 13

In No. 13 the first note of each slurred group retains the original accent, while the second note is given only one fourth of the volume

19

the first note received. If the original accent as given in No. 12 were retained when performing the melody in No. 13, it would sound incorrect to the ear accustomed to the proper interpretation.

When two notes are tied on the same degree of the staff, the figure is given a *bold* accent. When two notes are slurred on different degrees of the staff, the figure is given a *subdued* accent. In all cases where the *subdued* accent is used, the second note should be played with less volume than the first note. The extract given below illustrates this point nicely.

No. 14

In this melody, *bold* accent is used in the second and fourth measures because the two notes are tied on the same degree of the.staff.

If the same theme were written with the second note in the second and fourth measures either above or below the first note, we would have an excellent illustration of *subdued* accent. In this case, the second note should be played much softer than the first note in order to sound correct. This should be done even if the music is devoid of all marks of expression because the grammar of music calls for such treatment.

No. 15

Instructors and directors who know from practical experience how many good points are discovered in listening to fine singers, often advise close attention to the performances of the better vocal music. The phonograph or the radio are usually available and frequently afford excellent opportunities for listening to excellent vocal artists.

Many members of musical organizations are quite capable of singing or humming a popular well-known melody in fairly good style.

They do this naturally and with apparent ease. Right there, they have the proper cue to help them make rapid advancement in their musical endeavors. Frequently, however, in spite of their ability to carry a melody with correct tempo and in good style, when they take up their instruments, they seem to strive for effects that change the character of the music to such an extent that it is scarcely recognizable. Without a doubt, their enthusiasm for mastering the technique of their instruments suppresses their natural talents, and they are only concerned with playing all of the notes no matter how unmusical they may sound.

CHAPTER SIX

$\mathcal{T}$O interpret a melody correctly—to play or sing it in good style with the proper expression, it is necessary to know at a glance the really important notes of the melody and those that have been introduced in the composition as embellishments or ornamental notes.

The really important notes in a melody are those which cannot be dispensed with and still have the melody sound complete and satisfying. They usually occur on the beginning of a beat, although an exception to this rule occurs frequently in syncopated forms of music. These notes should receive emphasis, stress or accent.

The notes in a melody that are embellishments or ornamental notes should be played without emphasis—lighter or softer than the principal notes. Another point that is important to bear in mind is that it is well to shorten perceptibly the time value of the second note in a phrase which calls for *subdued* accent, as this will assist in reducing the accent on that note to a marked extent. If the melody set forth in No. 15 is played correctly it will sound as if it were written like this:

No. 16

So far these principles of accent have only been utilized with 2/4 figures. These same rules can be applied to any and all *tempi* met with

23

in music. An illustration of *bold* accent is given in the following *Allegro Marziale,* 4/4 movement:

No. 17

In No. 17, *bold* accent is used in the first, second, fourth, fifth, sixth and eighth measures. In No. 18, the same melody is employed using *subdued* accent. The change in accent is plainly marked.

No. 18

By carefully following the fundamentals set forth above as well as those regarding curtailment previously studied, the interpretation of this melody should sound as if it had really been written in this manner:

Allegro marziale

No. 19

Notice that all notes requiring *subdued* accent have been perceptibly shortened in time value; that the dotted eighth notes, as well as the quarter notes in the third and seventh measures, should be played shorter than written because this is a *staccato* passage in rapid tempo.

After a careful study of the foregoing principles followed by repeated practice of the excerpts set forth, many will naturally wonder just how this melody would have sounded if played without regard for the factors that govern good style and expression. Example No. 18 should be played as if it had been written as set forth in No. 19. Before they understood the correct interpretation, many would have played this *Allegro Marziale* as if it had been written like this:

No. 20

This example is not over emphasized in the least as any experienced musician will attest to. The greatest obstacle to correct interpretation usually lies in the fact that many are perfectly content to blow loudly, play as high as possible and make all the notes. Naturally, those who are satisfied with such indifferent performance will never enter the ranks of the finished players. They will never educate their ear to demand that which is grammatically correct and artistic. The longer they play with this incorrect conception, the more satisfied they become with their interpretation. Consequently, it becomes increasingly difficult for a teacher or experienced musician to correct their faulty playing. It is not an exaggeration to add that the best efforts of a musical organization can be marred or even ruined by the performance of one or more members who use bad style.

In No. 21, the omission of any note in the first two measures of this *Maestoso* movement will completely destroy the melodic line.

No. 21

However, in the last two measures, the melody still sounds quite complete and satisfactory when the eighth notes are entirely omitted. In this instance, the eighth notes in question are ornamental (notes of embellishment) and should receive less volume than is given to the notes occurring on the beat.

This same theme is given another treatment through the introduction of more notes of embellishment in the following excerpt:

No. 22

In this illustration enough time has been taken from each important or principal note to allow a full beat or count of ornamentation to follow. A marked accent is given to the first and third beats in each measure while the eighth notes are to be played lightly.

Still more notes are used to embellish this melody in No. 23. In this example, the triplets should be played more lightly than the ornamentations in the previous excerpt because there are more notes to each embellishment.

No. 23

The interpretation of a phrase containing grace notes is usually done in such a manner that they receive just about the proper volume and, of course, the passage sounds fairly well. Example No. 24 is another variation of the original melody, this time embellished through the introduction of grace notes.

No. 24

When performing a passage written in this manner, it is quite obvious that the large notes receive the most volume and the grace notes much less volume because it is plainly pictured to do so. On the other hand, the treatment of this melody usually suffers greatly if the grace notes are written out as large as the principal notes. In reality, there should be very little difference in the sound of this passage when it is played as written above or when it is written this way:

No. 25

When the sixteenth notes are written as large as the principal notes, many are inclined to play them correspondingly heavy with far more accent than they require. This is because they give little or no attention to the contrast necessary between the important notes that comprise the melody and the ornamental notes which are added to it as embellishments.

After the above illustrations, the true interpretation of the melody as written in No. 26 should not be difficult to grasp. The sixteenth notes are in reality three notes of embellishment—or grace notes—and their tonal volume should be reduced accordingly. They should not be pounded out just because they are printed as large as the quarter notes preceding them.

No. 26

When this melody is correctly interpreted, all of the stress should be placed on the half notes, and it should sound as if it were written this way:

No. 27

In No. 28, the length of the principal notes has been greatly reduced so that the extra sixteenth notes comprising the ornamentation could be introduced. In such phrases the eighth notes and quarter notes usually receive about four times the volume of the sixteenth notes.

No. 28

In the final illustration used in this chapter, the principal notes of the original melody are well sustained, considering the great number of notes embraced by the ornamentations between them. In the first measure, the accent occurs only upon the first and third beats. All of the thirty-second notes should be played very lightly so that they may be played swiftly. It is evident that these thirty-second notes are to be treated as if they were grace notes occurring between the original half notes in the melody.

No. 29

Those who have acquired the ability of playing softly usually find the above passage easy to execute. The fingering is purely mechanical and can be mastered with practice; in most cases the obstacle does not lie in that direction. Those who encounter difficulty in playing such a passage correctly are frequently over-blowing or over-exerting themselves. In their eagerness to master a particular phrase that is giving them trouble, they will emphasize it. The more difficulty they have with the passage, the louder they play it, whereas this is the exact place they should be using their softest tones.

No one can run fast and stamp on the ground with his heels at the same time. Speed will obliterate accent. Therefore, it is essential to play softly whenever there are many notes to be performed to each beat or fraction thereof. The more extended the embellishment the more lightly it should be performed. To play with expression, the performer should practice softly and slowly, at the same time concentrating on the true valuation of each note in its relationship to all of the other notes.

CHAPTER SEVEN

𝒯HE best efforts of any performer to render a melody correctly (with intelligent and well-placed emphasis) are of little avail if his tones are rough and harsh or tend to have a snarl in them. The definition of the term *legato* is understood by most players. They are certain that they will not have a great deal of trouble with such a passage. When instructed to play a phrase in *legato* style, many will try to produce a tone of good quality and smoothness. Generally, their rendition is faulty and cannot be compared with singing, but to them the passage sounds well played. When, however, they are asked to play a passage *staccato*, their complete lack of understanding glares forth. Many musicians and teachers, after asking what the term *staccato* really means, have been astounded at the answers they have received. One young player will answer: "Why it means to spit them out," while another will say, "Tongue them good and hard," or "It means to cut them off." If the instructor receives such a reply, he realizes that the tonal quality of a *staccato* passage will be utterly destroyed when the student tries to interpret it because of his misunderstanding of the meaning of the term. First of all, the correct definition of the term should be studied and memorized.

STACCATO: *Detached, separated; a direction to perform a passage in an abrupt, disconnected manner.*

The above definition carries no suggestion or advances no rule to destroy the tonal quality of a passage when it is played *staccato*. The words "detached, separated" clearly explain that the notes are to be played with rests after them; each note should take up the time value given it but a part of that time shall be given to tone and the balance to rest—or silence.

A passage played *staccato* should have the same good tonal quality that is given to a *legato* melody. The trained musician does not change the tonal quality of his playing when he is directed to play either of these styles.

Those who define the term *staccato* with the words "It means to spit them out," usually produce a snappy tone (or noise) with a pronounced snarl to it whenever they perform a *staccato* passage. This is because they force the tip of their tongue against the front upper teeth and lip, harden the muscles of their throat, press the breath heavily against the tongue and suddenly release it, in this way "spitting" an amount of compressed air into the mouthpiece of the instrument which produced the snappy tone referred to.

The next definition, "It means to cut them off," seems to demonstrate the belief that each tone must be cut off abruptly even if it is necessary to sacrifice tonal quality to accomplish this end. Those who give this definition of *staccato* are usually the ones who end all *staccato* notes with a clearly articulated "UT." It seems almost needless to add that such an articulation will destroy the ending of any and every tone made upon an instrument.

The last definition, "Tongue them hard," seems to indicate a combination of all the incorrect methods given in the two preceding paragraphs in playing a passage *staccato*.

Many experience their principal difficulty when they have to execute a *staccato* passage composed of eighth notes or sixteenth notes. At this point, it usually becomes evident that they change to an incorrect method of attack and manner of sustaining and releasing each tone. After studying the following illustration, this is readily understood and easily explained. The melody in No. 30 is composed of eight measures taken from the strain of a march. Because it is a march figure, the notes should be played *staccato* (separated) as this style of playing will best suggest a body of marching men.

No. 30

Many seem to meet with no difficulties when playing this melody. In most cases, their attack is fairly good and they release each tone naturally without contracting the throat muscles. They do not show a tendency to end each tone with an "UT" and usually place the required rest after each note, so that there is a fair degree of separation.

In the playing of *staccato* on stringed instruments, the wrist should never be used; rather, the *staccato* should be made directly from the elbow. In a passage of some length the arm will have an involuntary tendency to stiffen, and this in itself is good, inasmuch as it will aid in the production of a clean, vigorous tone. Many individuals have tried to play this type of bowing with their wrist; however, the results are anything but satisfactory for neither strength, firmness nor rapidity can be developed by this manner of playing.

The above example is usually played as if it were written like this, which is good and correct:

No. 31

Up to this point very few ever encounter serious trouble. However, when this same melody is written so as to be played twice as fast—as if it were embraced in four measures instead of eight—and the *staccato* style of playing is required throughout, many will immediately change their manner of articulation. It is then that the experienced musician refers to them as a "Tutter." As is frequently the case, many are not aware of this change for the worse in their rendition and do not realize that the attentive listener at once detects the difference. To demonstrate this point, play No. 31 and follow it immediately with the melody in No. 32. Compare the manner of playing both themes and notice if the attack, release and quality of all tones are alike. If they are not alike, practice these two excerpts until the effect of both is similar.

No. 32

After mastering the two previous examples, further development of this technique is possible by practicing this melody still faster, retaining the *staccato* style of playing and striving to do so without sacrificing the quality, attack or release of each tone. In the following example the melody is reduced to four beats contained in two measures:

No. 33

After the foregoing, it should be obvious that a short note must be played with the same care as a long note. If both are to be played with the same volume, the half note and the sixteenth note should differ only in the length of the tone. The sixteenth note should receive the same careful attack, the same tone quality and release as does the whole, half or quarter note. With diligent practice, the melody in example No. 30 can be played so rapidly that two measures are played to the count of one. Of course, when it is played at this tempo, the melody will sound exactly as it has been written in No. 33.

When experiencing any trouble in playing the notes of a *staccato* passage in a detached manner, practice very slowly at first. It is often best to play only one note and then stop, play the next note and stop, and so on, stopping a full second after each note if necessary. If this phase of *staccato* playing is causing difficulty, this system of practice will soon tend to correct it.

Rapid advancement towards playing a true and perfect *staccato* can be obtained by repeated diligent practice in the correct manner. Merely playing an instrument for years will not develop many musicianly qualities unless the performer is aware of his faults, and attempts to overcome them. To find out at just what degree of speed the proper execution of *staccato* begins to fail or at what point the change from correct to incorrect style takes place, practice the following example according to the instructions given.

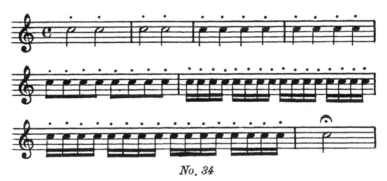

No. 34

The prime object is to play all the notes that appear in example No. 34 with good attack, the best possible tone, proper release, and to separate each tone with a rest. Start the half notes slowly (separating all of them), and increase the speed regularly. When the first of the quarter notes is played there should be no perceptible change in the length of the last half note and the first quarter note. Continue to increase the speed of the quarter notes (always separating them) so that the first eighth notes will sound like fast quarter notes. Continue to increase the speed while playing the eighth notes so that they will meet the sixteenth notes without any noticeable change in the tempo.

If this is done correctly, the player will feel that he is starting on slow half notes and accelerating them to such an extent that at the finish he is playing them so fast that they are sixteenth notes. The whole procedure may be compared with the dropping of a rubber ball and watching it bounce, or to the steadily increasing speed in the exhaust of a locomotive, when it starts slowly with a heavy load and gradually gains speed. Naturally the tone should gradually decrease in volume as the speed of the notes increases.

There are various styles and grades of *staccato* used in the numerous compositions most musicians are called upon to play at different times. The wide separation of tones that one melody might require to make it sound well, may make the next selection sound ridiculous. A close study of interpretations by experienced performers will aid in perfecting proper judgment along these lines.

The points stressed in the foregoing chapters have been selected with one object in view. If these principles and their application are practiced painstakingly and frequently, many will begin to notice a tendency to play grammatically and with good expression. They will soon appreciate the seemingly unimportant little things which make the rendition of a composition either good, bad or indifferent. It is earnestly hoped that those who study and practice these basic concepts of musical expression will, through their mastery, develop themselves to the degree of perfection they desire to obtain.

CHAPTER EIGHT

*W*HILE the faults common to many are most evident when they perform a passage in *staccato* style, usually a great deal can also be done to improve their *legato* playing. The definition of the term should be studied and memorized.

LEGATO: Smooth, together; a direction to perform a passage in a flowing connected manner.

From this definition it is obvious that once the first note of a *legato* phrase has been sounded, the tone should not stop; nor should one tone become separated from another until the end of the phrase is reached or a rest occurs.

As previously stated, there are many styles and grades of *staccato*, but there is only one kind of *legato*—connected, unbroken tones—never separated. As soon as the notes of a *legato* phrase are separated they become a form of *staccato*.

If the notes in a *legato* phrase are attacked with the same force that is applied to a *staccato* passage, the tones produced will usually be too harsh. The first note in a *legato* passage should be started by putting the tongue well in front, to the point of the upper front teeth, similar to playing a *staccato* note. The tone should continue steadily after this attack, and for the second and all succeeding tones after the first one the tongue should touch the roof of the mouth about a half of an inch in back of the upper teeth similar to the motion used to produce a whispered "DU." It is this articulation that should be used throughout the playing of a *legato* phrase. When a stop in the tone is made for a rest or the taking of breath, the tongue should start the new tone by again being placed well forward in the mouth for the attack. After the first note has been attacked, the succeeding notes are produced as before with the whispered articulation, "DU." To many there is nothing new in this explanation. However, it is quite possible that they may have produced tones in *legato* playing which are entirely

35

faulty and unmusical in spite of the fact that they use this method. Here again it seems necessary to add that careful and intelligent practice will bring about the desired result.

Those playing stringed instruments will find that *legato* playing is the supreme test of a performer's ability to produce a smooth, flowing tone. Changes from down bow to up bow and vice versa should be imperceptible, and made with the arm, and not with the wrist. The bow itself should be drawn parallel with the bridge of a stringed instrument, and when playing a phrase calling for a moderate amount of tone, the bow should be at a place on the string half-way between the bridge and the fingerboard; when playing softer, the bow should be drawn closer to the fingerboard, and when playing louder, it should find its place closer to the bridge. Long, steady bows should be drawn by those intent on developing a pure, *legato* style of playing, and in practicing such bowing, equalized pressure should be placed on the bow from the frog to its tip.

While the playing of a song in *legato* style is considered by many authorities to be the supreme test for the student, the novice seldom seems to worry about the interpretation of a *legato* phrase because he knows the correct definition of the term. When given a song to play he usually proceeds in a manner which is unnatural and unpleasant in spite of all the confidence he has in himself. Although he may be well satisfied with the results, not so the more experienced musician who knows that *legato* or song playing tests the performer's ability to the utmost. He seldom worries about a phrase which contains a large number of notes requiring rapid execution, but when he reaches a *legato* passage, he will instantly put forth his best efforts to give a smooth, flowing performance.

In order to become proficient in the rapid execution of phrases containing a large number of notes, it is necessary to practice scales, grupettos and broken chords in the various keys. This phase of playing is almost entirely mechanical. Song playing *(legato)* requires a great deal more from the performer. The correct practice of *legato* phrases calls for mental application, pure tone and intelligently placed accent.

A song is not well played merely because it is played "from the heart." When a *legato* passage is well executed it is because the performer is using his knowledge to place the correct accent on exactly the right notes. His experience tells him that one note should be played strongly and the next two or three softly. If he did not use this important knowledge, his rendition would certainly be ungrammatical.

It is of no avail to practice songs, as many are often advised to do, unless it is clearly understood just what is to be accomplished through such a procedure. Blowing or bowing songs hour after hour will not develop proficient effective interpretation unless the performer knows what *legato* playing sounds like in advance and strives to duplicate it. The mistakes committed in attempting song or *legato* playing are about the same in every case, a few of them being as follows:

The attack is too hard or too sharp.

The tongue is too slow in touching the roof of the mouth and retiring. This causes the tones to separate because the tongue, being slow, interferes with the passage of the breath.

Not sufficient breath is taken for each passage, especially after the first phrase has been played. Breath is essential; therefore learn to take as much as is needed.

When a deep breath is taken it is not controlled properly; consequently the tone is too loud immediately after it.

The pointed notes (dotted eighth, quarter and half notes) are taken too softly and invariably diminish in volume before they end (whether they are so marked or not).

The notes that should be of short duration (eighth and sixteenth notes) are played entirely too strong in comparison to the long notes, thereby creating a sing-song monotonous style.

Each phrase is played with the same volume instead of accenting it naturally along the lines of conversation.

The use of a throat or stomach tremolo or *vibrato*, on all of the long notes hardens the muscles of the throat and tongue, so that the quality of the tone produced is anything but musical.

In the case of stringed instruments, players fail to draw their bow parallel with the bridge of their instruments; hence, the tone produced is rough and scratchy, rather than smooth and pure.

Some *andantes* sound very sad when performed too slowly; others sound just as poorly because they are played too fast and too much in the style of a march.

These are a few of the more common mistakes, all of which can be avoided by observing others, careful practice and concentration.

Correct expression cannot be given to a *legato* passage unless the player can articulate and breathe perfectly. Practice of the following examples according to the instructions layed out will rapidly improve the ability to perform a good *legato*.

No. 35

In starting the tone given in example No. 35, do not harden or stiffen the muscles at the root of the tongue. Take a deep breath, place the tongue very gently at the point of the upper teeth and drop it into the mouth and at the same time force the breath through the instrument. Throughout the four measures continue this tone striving to make it the best quality possible, either *piano, mezzo-piano* or *forte*. The volume of the tone should not be diminished or increased at any point during the playing of the entire excerpt. Count slowly and steadily and stop the tone by shutting off the supply of air at the lungs, not with the tongue or with the throat muscles. As soon as this procedure has been mastered, continue with the next example.

No. 36

In practicing No. 36, take a deep breath and start the first note in the same manner as in the previous example. Without stopping the tone in the least, the tongue should ascend to the roof of the mouth and touch it gently about a half inch in back of the upper teeth while inaudibly pronouncing the syllable "DU." For each succeeding note it will have to ascend quickly to the same spot and retire just as quickly. It is of utmost importance that the tongue does not dwell for any length of time at the roof of the mouth. Notice that the tone will not stop at all if the tongue is nimble enough, merely giving the slight articulation "DU." Perhaps the easiest way to explain the action the tongue should take is to say it should bounce to its position and back again.

Some *legato* melodies require more pronounced and clearer articulation than others. The closer the point of the tongue advances to a position between the lips, the harder will be the attack when it retires. In the same way, the farther back in the roof of the mouth that the tongue ascends, the softer or more delicate will be the attack. It is necessary to practice until control of every style of attack necessary to interpret melodies correctly has been obtained.

To get the greatest amount of benefit from the practice of No. 36, play very slowly at first, as if the exercise were written in half notes. After repeated practice, increase the speed of playing until the passage sounds as though it were written in eighth notes and then in sixteenth notes. Of course, the same good tone and soft attack must be retained throughout. When ready to proceed further, try this same style of articulation on the following example as well as several familiar melodies which require *legato* style interpretation.

No. 37

Although this little song is marked to be played softly, it does not mean that every note is to be played with the same volume of tone. This brings us to the subject of emphasis in *legato* playing and its bearing on expression in music as considered in the next chapter.

CHAPTER NINE

*J*UDGING the weight of an object by lifting it with the hand is an accomplishment which some people have acquired, and one in which they may become very apt through frequent practice.

Volume in tone is judged by the ear alone and it takes consistent practice along this line to develop the necessary proficiency. Some who have had wide experience as performers have never given the matter a single serious thought. To say that they lack expression in their playing is the usual way of explaining their uninteresting renditions. Criticism usually has very little effect on this type of player as they have become satisfied with their results. Usually they give plenty of volume (often too much) to each note played and they have no desire to produce the tones with the marked contrast necessary to make their interpretation of the melody flowing.

It is impractical to include on a printed copy of music all of the characters needed to instruct the player as to the relative volume of all the notes to be played in a passage. This knowledge must come through experience, based on the study and application of the principles which result in good style and expression.

The vocalist uses the words of a song as well as the melody to attract and retain the attention of the audience. The next time the efforts of a really good singer are scrutinized, notice the contrasts in volume given to the different tones and how marked and pronounced these contrasts stand out (depending upon the nature of the composition).

If the singer resorts to the use of these high contrasts of volume in the rendition of a song, it is equally essential that the instrumentalist pattern his interpretation of a melody in the same fashion. The latter has only the melody with which to entertain, whereas the vocalist uses both words and music. For this reason alone, the instrumentalist should color the melody with even greater contrasts than the vocalist uses.

The schooled instrumentalist readily understands and profits by the facts which have been explained in the above paragraphs. The principles that govern emphasis in relation to playing in good style should make it possible to rapidly analyze an entire melody, as well as each phrase thereof, and play the same with expression while reading at sight. To those who have never studied the principles of musical expression, this feat seems quite a difficult accomplishment.

For practice take example No. 37, given in the preceding chapter, and make a complete analysis of it, phrase by phrase. Do this thoroughly, marking plainly the relative volume to be given to each note, and analyzing the necessary increase in volume of some notes and the decrease in volume of others. By similarly applying these principles to other melodies, the sing-song or humdrum results will be eliminated. The following is the first phrase of the melody.

No. 38

First, observe the tempo in which this phrase is to be played—sixty beats to the minute. This tempo should be increased gradually until it reaches seventy-two and then gradually reduced to sixty. These gradual changes have a great deal to do with describing the emotions pictured in the melody. The figures immediately over the notes describe the relative volume which should be given to them when played or sung. Notice that the first three notes are to be played with steadily increasing volume, while the last note in the first measure is to be played lightly in comparison to the others—because it is a note that follows a dotted note and must be played unaccented. The climax of the phrase is reached in the second measure and for this reason the eighth notes in this measure should be played with increasing volume. It is also effective to dwell slightly on the highest eighth note—the "D." In the third measure the notes should be given less volume than in the second measure. This is because the third and fourth measures are in the nature of an answer to the first subject and are therefore meek in character to afford a contrast. In sustaining the three beats in the fourth measure care must be taken that the tone at this point does not diminish in volume. The third count should be sustained as long as the first or second count. In fact, the phrase will sound even better if the tone volume in this case is increased instead of diminished. Now study the second phrase which follows:

No. 39

In example No. 39, a radical change must necessarily be made in the harmony. This suggests the emotion of excitement—therefore the tempo must be faster. However, as the harmony returns to the dominant of the original key at the close of this phrase, the tempo should gradually slacken again. The climax of this phrase occurs on the third count of the third measure; therefore, the performer could dwell upon this note a little with good effect. Observe all of the changes in emphasis in this phrase while practicing it many times. Keep in mind that the melody should not be broken between any of the tones in this excerpt. The tone should be as continuous as if the entire melody had been marked to be slurred. The attack should be very soft, using the *legato* accent throughout. This point must be understood or it will become habitual to sharply attack the notes in song playing. The third phrase follows:

No. 40

Here the melody has modulated to the key of A flat. This suggests still greater agitation. Therefore, this phrase must be played much faster—as fast as one hundred and twelve beats to the minute—and softly, with a gradual *ritenendo* at the end. Then too, in such cases a change must be made in the volume of the tone to conform to the abrupt change in the key. As the melody flows faster, play softer using less emphasis, until the end of the phrase where the tempo again gets slower and in consequence the accent should become more marked. When practicing this phrase observe the tempo and the emphasis markings very closely.

No. 41

The phrase in No. 41 gradually works its way back to the original key (through its dominant harmony). In such cases, the melody should be played stronger in order to impress the listener with this change. It should also be played slower to demonstrate the sincerity and ultimate objective. These are precisely the same methods an orator would use when he returns to his original text. The elocutionist well knows the value of this maneuver and utilizes it with good results.

No. 42

The phrase in No. 42 is the same as the first phrase in example No. 38 and receives the same treatment as to tempi and emphasis. The only exception occurs in the last measure. Observe the great volume with which the last measure is played so as to anticipate and establish the entrance into the next phrase. If this is not done the extreme power required at the opening of the last phrase would be too abrupt and sound terrorizing. Many well-meaning performers attain this end without meaning to. This introduces the final measures which should be played in this manner:

No. 43

The above phrase is the most difficult of all to interpret. The first measure contains the real climax of the entire melody. Notice that the tempo is much slower than for any of the preceding phrases, and it grows gradually slower to the finish. Also notice that the first three notes are to be taken with ten points of accent. The little straight lines with dots under them which have been placed over the first three notes mean that they are to be strongly emphasized, and that they are to be slightly separated to mark the emotion of great sincerity in the melody. Be sure that the eighth note following the dotted quarter note is played unaccented. A gradual *diminuendo* is called for in the second measure as the melody descends. After the fifth eighth note in the second measure play very *legato* until the finish, observing the relative volume of the notes as marked. The last tone should be sustained for three full counts which should be much slower than the preceding ones. Guard against the common fault of ending an *andante* too abruptly by sounding the last note its proper value—three full counts.

While it is true that no two musicians will interpret a melody precisely alike as to the emphasis and shading, it is also true that to a great extent, they will agree as to the varying tempi and climaxes in a melody. If only half of the suggestions given for the playing of each phrase in this melody are used the monotonous sing-song style, so common to many renditions, will certainly be avoided.

CHAPTER TEN

*A*S mentioned before, when the vocalist interprets a song, he has a great advantage over the instrumentalist. The words around which the music is written point out the necessary *crescendos, diminuendos,* climaxes, etc., and make it a comparatively easy matter for the vocalist to give expression to his rendition. However, the instrumentalist must rely on his own ability to play a melody, devoid of words, intelligently and with proper expression so that it tells a story. This brings to mind the oft reiterated statement that the player must do more than blow, finger and play in time and tune in order to play with expression.

Sometimes a melody will contain an aggressive subject which is followed by an answer that is still more aggressive. Then again an aggressive phrase may be followed by several measures which suggest a meek and subdued answer. To play a melody with the proper expression requires as much care and thought as the delivery of the spoken sentence by an orator. This point was very clearly and graphically illustrated at the beginning of this treatise (see page 3). It would be just as erroneous for the instrumentalist to play a dotted note and the note following it with equal tone volume, as it would be for a public speaker to give undue accent or emphasis to all such words as *a, and* or *the.* This treatment also applies to a phrase in which notes of short duration occur between sustained tones. An effort to play in good style will be unsuccessful if the tone volume of the short notes is not properly diminished.

As stated before, an aggressive subject may be followed by an answer which is still more aggressive in character. The following excerpt illustrates this point:

No. 44

The subject in the first two measures of the above melody is rather pompous and bombastic in character. The answer to this subject as found in the third and fourth measures demands an increase in tone volume because of its suggested aggressiveness. The reason for this lies in the fact that the melody in the third and fourth measures ascends to a climax and therefore plainly indicates that a more dramatic interpretation is called for.

In the next illustration, a situation is introduced in which an aggressive subject is followed by a meek subdued answer. This is the same melody that was used in No. 44.

No. 45

Notice that no change has been made in the first phrase except in the eighth notes that lead to the answer. The notes which comprise the answer plainly indicate that they should be played meekly—in a subdued manner. The melody very clearly descends, is devoid of all notes requiring marked emphasis, and therefore demands a subdued style of treatment.

Examination of the two preceding excerpts reveals them to be entirely devoid of marks of expression and without tempo indications. The knowledge absorbed in the preceding chapters should aid in applying the accent to the melody exactly where it belongs. To experiment with the tempo for this melody, enlist the aid of a metronome. First set the pendulum of the metronome to beat 60 counts per minute while playing, humming or whistling the melody. Notice this tempo sounds entirely too slow, that the melody is robbed of all its pompousness and is dull and lifeless. Next set the pendulum much faster, about 92 beats per minute, and repeat the melody at this speed. There is now an immediate change for the better. To experiment still further, set the metronome to beat 100, 112, 126 and 132 counts per minute. At each trial observe that the results sound lighter and at the highest speeds mentioned almost insipid, but that the tempo of 112 beats per minute fits the melody perfectly. When played at that rate of speed, it suggests a *Maestoso* or *Grandioso* movement. Having established a satisfactory tempo, the accents should now be placed where they belong. The first theme (No. 44), because of its aggressive character and still more aggressive answer, should be marked this way:

No. 46

In analyzing the markings in the above example, notice that the notes following the dotted notes are to be played with less volume than the dotted notes. The down-beat, or first count, of the fourth measure is to be played with less accent than the second and third counts. In this case the second note should be given preference over the first and the volume should be greater.

Similarly examine the second melody given in No. 45. The change made in this passage must be understood if it is to be correctly analyzed and marked. The first seven beats should receive the same aggressive treatment as was given to them in No. 46. However, the answer is completely different in character. Because of this change, the last part of this phrase demands a somewhat slower tempo, much less volume and a subdued and pleading style. If this excerpt were used as the opening theme of an overture, it would probably be played something like this:

No. 47

The example in No. 48, incorporates an entirely different situation. Here the subject contains little more than three counts, whereas the answer thereto is given in a more extended form. If this melody were performed exactly as it appears, without introducing marked emphasis on some of the notes and subduing the volume of others, it would sound weak, insipid and meaningless. To demonstrate this point, examine the following excerpt closely and hum, sing or play it exactly as it is written.

No. 48

Similarly, examine the melody as shown in No. 49. Here it has been dressed up with the proper marks for tempi and accent marks have been placed in their respective places in accordance with the principles already discussed.

No. 49

Notice that the first measure is given very forceful treatment suitable to its innate character. The eighth note that follows the half note should be played softly (with *subdued* accent). The pause *(fermata)* over the rest in this measure should receive careful consideration. It should be held for two or even three counts so that it will create suspense and expectation in the mind of the listener. The *Lento* which follows should be played exactly as suggested by the marking—softly and pleadingly. The second half of this excerpt is the same as the first and should be treated in a similar manner. Play or sing this melody several times using all of the marks of expression and tempo which have been added in No. 49. By following these markings closely, the melody will have a positive character and will say something very definite. This time it will not sound lifeless and meaningless, but should be like an interesting conversation, the first party speaking in terms of excitement and anger while the replies are subdued and pleading in manner.

To color all melodies with such sharp contrasts as has been recommended in the above example would be in extremely bad taste, in fact in many instances such colorings and contrasts would border on the ridiculous.

To play with good taste and intelligence, it is highly essential to study the character of every composition before it is performed and incorporate in its interpretation the various principles of expression and accent. Often a teacher or director instructs a student to play with expression exactly as the composer intended. The efforts of the performer often end in dire results when he follows these instructions without first analyzing the composition intelligently and applying the correct accent and good style. Sometimes when a performer strictly adheres to the expression marks which appear on printed music the results are very satisfactory, but just as often they are very sad. An incident which occurred in the life of a young composer and band leader illustrates this assertion.

The composer referred to had written numerous compositions for band and orchestra, several of which had been published. Some of them were quite well-known and were played extensively. On his programs he usually featured several of his own compositions and whenever possible, included his latest published number. Several times he experienced the supreme satisfaction of hearing another band, an organization composed of excellently trained musicians play his latest march. Although he was highly pleased and flattered, he was puzzled, because he had to admit that the march sounded very different—even better— than he had intended when he composed it. On one occasion he sought out the bandmaster and said to him: "Why, you play that new march of mine even better than I imagined it would sound."

The bandmaster replied: "Certainly; I heard your band play it. They lack expression, accent and emphasis. In fact, your men play it the way it looks."

One of the strains of the march referred to was similar to the following excerpt, and the composer's band played it exactly as it was printed.

No. 50

When this same strain was played by the experienced band, the effect was entirely different, because routine practice and intelligently placed accent made the theme sound as if it had been written in this manner:

No. 51

Here is food for thought indeed. When the rendition of a piece of music—just as it is printed—is placed side by side with the interpretation of a trained, intelligent musician it is like comparing the mongrel with the thoroughbred dog. They may both be healthy, active animals of the same size and weight, but the thoroughbred has more clearly defined features, greater refinement, nobler character and will make a more lasting impression on those who see him.

CHAPTER ELEVEN

*O*F marked importance in the study of expression in music is the art of playing a good accompaniment. Frequently, accompaniment parts (especially in bands) are left to the tender mercies of beginners or those who do not possess any ability whatsoever as to execution and tone. Those who cannot handle a melody part proficiently are scarcely competent of playing an accompaniment to others. Only an experienced first chair player can appreciate how an accompaniment should sound and how essential it is that its volume is subdued at all times in relation to the melody.

In the interpretation of afterbeats, great care must be exercised to see that the tones do not equal in volume the tones that are played on the beat by the basses. This is a point that is often ignored by accompaniment players; in fact, they often perform these accompaniment parts in such a manner that the volume exceeds that of the basses. It is not always the horns and secondary cornets that commit this error of over-blowing on accompaniment parts. Very often a marching band will have several strong armed trombone players in the front rank. At one time or another, everyone has experienced the painful incident of hearing a composition executed in this fashion:

No. 52

This passage is the introduction and part of the first strain to a march. Unquestionably, the trombonists played this excerpt exactly as

51

it looks—every note *ff*—unisons, solos and the afterbeat accompani-
ments. It is needless to add that they used very poor judgment in their
interpretation and in so doing spoiled the balance of the entire band.
The unison passage at the opening of the introduction was quite correctly played *forte*. The same holds true of the solo passage in the third
and fourth measures of the first strain. However, the afterbeats occurring in the last measure of the introduction and in the first two measures of the strain should have been greatly reduced in volume. They
should correspond in volume with that of the horns. Such an interpretation would have shown experienced judgment on the part of the
trombone section.

Accompanying parts occurring on the accented beats should
equal in volume the tones being used by the basses. Accompanying
parts occurring in the form of afterbeats should invariably be subdued
in volume in comparison with the bass notes occurring on the beat.
The smooth balanced effect which strict observance of this practice
helps bring about would amaze the members of many bands.

There are some trombone players who do not know how to interpret correctly the march theme given in No. 53. In most cases, they
will play every note with an equal amount of volume, playing none of
them softly (unless they run out of breath).

No. 53

The passage in the above illustration contains both accompaniment and counter melodies. The whole notes in the first two measures
should be played rather softly—subdued. The third, fourth, fifth and
sixth measures consist of a counter-melody which is given in the form
of an echo to the regular melody. This passage distinctly calls for
character and individuality; consequently, the measures referred to
should receive proportionate volume. The last two measures are in the
form of afterbeats and, as such, should receive very little volume, even
though they occur in a *forte* passage. Some young aspiring trombone
players do not realize how important it is that this variation in volume
be given to different measures so very close together. This passage
should be executed as if it had been written as follows:

No. 54

This brings back once more the statement which has occurred several times previously. Because it is impossible to incorporate, in a printed piece of music, all the markings necessary to indicate correctly the relative volume and length of each note, the surest way to play with good expression is to learn the principles of accent—the grammar of music—and how to apply them with intelligence and good judgment.

It is amusing at times to hear a lone trumpeter or cornetist in an orchestra or band poke out the afterbeats in a simple waltz figure. Whereas he is supposed to be playing an accompaniment that will strengthen the harmony, he is really making his loudly-played little afterbeats cover the melody and spoil the combined efforts of the group. The trumpeter who plays all the tones of the following waltz theme with equal volume, even though it is marked to be played *forte,* will not assist the orchestra one iota in obtaining the dreamy effect this style of composition demands.

No. 55

It is quite as necessary for the second and third cornet (or trumpet) players as well as any other accompaniment or harmony player in an organization to know just when it is necessary to bring out their parts. In passages similar to the one in No. 56, the second and third cornet players have the melody in unison with the First Cornet for the first two measures, therefore they should play it with the same volume used by the lead instruments.

No. 56

In the third and fourth measures of the strain, the trumpets should brilliantly assert themselves so as to secure the best effect. The Fanfare and the sustained tones in the first four measures are followed by a succession of notes that suggest accompaniment—not solo—and these notes must be played in a subdued manner.

Do not overlook the horn players as they too usually merit some criticism. This section requires careful attention if there is to be a good harmonious foundation to the organization. An experienced director once said: "I don't particularly want to hear you horn players, but I shall miss you if you drop a single note." The horn section should usually play the after-beats in an accompaniment strain with about one-half the volume that the basses use on the beat and should at all times use a good intonation.

Second violin and viola players, when playing afterbeats in the orchestra, should do so with a firm, decisive stroke of the bow. Just a few inches of bow, near the center of the stick, should be used for playing music of this type, but there should be sufficient pressure through the thumb and first three fingers of the right hand to result in a tone of full, solid proportions.

A casual suggestion directed to the average bass player may not be amiss while on this subject. A really good Bassist recognizes his definite responsibility in a concert organization. He cannot assist the ensemble with a countless monotonous rendition on his instrument and consider it as part of an intelligent musical accompaniment. While the bass part is usually written on the accent beats, it is sure to sound monotonous if the volume is the same on all tones. Dotted notes, as well as notes that are foreign to the key in which the part is written, should receive especial emphasis or accent. To illustrate this point, the following passage has been taken from the first strain of a standard march:

No. 57

To interpret this passage correctly, the bass player will have to give especial emphasis to the half notes in the second and seventh measures. If these notes are played with the same volume that is given to the surrounding quarter notes, the result will be anything but a correct musical accompaniment.

To give a composition an intelligent and musical rendition, it is just as important for the performers of the accompanying parts to study and observe the rules for playing in good style as it is for the instrumentalists who play the melody parts. One player, who gives a careless, faulty rendition of his part can mar the best efforts of an entire organization.

CHAPTER TWELVE

*I*N an earlier chapter, reference was made to the numerous inexpensive opportunities which are available to the student and musician to hear and study the performances of the world's greatest singers, instrumentalists and musical organizations.

Almost all educators and musicians agree that listening to good interpretations by fine musicians is an excellent source of inspiration and education. Because it is often costly and inconvenient to attend concerts and recitals, the radio and phonograph offer inexpensive and easily accessible means of listening to the interpretations of the very best music by artists and organizations of the highest calibre.

The medium which affords the finest array of musical talent at the least expense is the radio. Weekly there are broadcast from the large urban centers, innumerable fine programs of diversified nature. Many of them are sent over the large networks of stations and can be heard in the remotest rural communities as well as the smaller cities and towns, thus making it possible for everyone to enjoy them. For many seasons, one of the outstanding Opera companies in this country has been on the air every Saturday. Close attention to one of their performances would at some point illustrate each and every principle given in this book, for only by experienced understanding and observance of expression and emphasis could all of the performers (soloists, chorus and orchestra) combine and produce a well-balanced, effective musical rendition.

The phonograph offers an almost inexhaustible supply of recordings which should prove a lasting inspiration to all listeners. The records can be played again and again so that detailed study can be centered on difficult passages which require careful shading, correct emphasis, *crescendo* and *diminuendo*, as well as one of the most important features of solo and ensemble playing—*tempo rubato.*

55

The fine quality of the present day high fidelity recordings gives representations of great artists in every field of music. Some recordings exist of almost every outstanding artist on every important instrument —piano, violin, cello, clarinet, trumpet, trombone and many others. Too much cannot be said on the subject of listening to and studying the interpretations of the finest musicians through this medium.

Many schools now own recording equipment while some of the present day radio and phonograph combinations also boast recording and play-back devices. These machines are of infinite assistance to the student and teacher who use them. After having listened repeatedly to a good recording and diligently and conscientiously practiced the composition, a player can, by means of these machines, make a very inexpensive recording of his own rendition and compare it with that of the artist. In a similar manner, both small and large groups can be inspired and guided to better and more musical performances.

Once more it seems advisable to call attention to the importance of ease in tone production. If it is necessary to blow hard or play loudly to sound a tone, it will be impossible to play with expression as an incorrect system of tone production often prevents reducing the volume in passages which demand such treatment. While this fault is common to many, an examination of the renditions given by finished performers reveals that they experience no great difficulty in playing *sotto voce* (in an undertone). This allows the climaxes to sound forceful and brilliant without undue volume and consequent roughness. An eminent trumpet player once said, "It is never necessary to play noisily. Anyone can play loudly. Artists only can play softly and well."

It should always be remembered that playing with expression or in good style consists of especially emphasized tones and well placed climaxes. A good tone is of great importance; however, it is possible to play with excellent tonal quality and faultless execution, and still play in poor style because of badly placed emphasis and accent.

While only a minority of the members of the bands and orchestras in the thousands of schools throughout the country are desirous of becoming professional musicians, many are interested in participating in the contests and festivals held in their locality. There are today really serious-minded players who desire to become artistic and proficient musicians and who are willing to study and practice to attain this end. To this group the suggestions contained in the foregoing chapters should prove of especial value if they are closely studied and practiced.

It will not suffice for the player to admit that the principles of playing with expression are of value and then ignore them when he plays a number. These fundamentals must be reviewed and rehearsed until it becomes as natural to use them in playing as it is to use good grammar in speaking. It is well to remember that what very often appears to be an unimportant part of the composition, is the exact place where the experienced performer strives his hardest.

The Director of a band or orchestra can also profit greatly by studying the rendition of a fine organist. By analyzing the contrasts and tonal balances of such a performance and striving to get these same effects at the subsequent rehearsals of his organization, he will eventually improve the group as a whole. One or two trials will seldom bring about the desired results; it takes perseverance and hard work to accomplish this end.

Many who possess copies of the previous edition of this work, have expressed its value to them. Some have found it well worth their while to refer to it from time to time and refresh their memory. While it is not necessary to do this frequently once these principles have been mastered, it will not be amiss to check back occasionally by reviewing a chapter or two of this volume.

If the principles outlined herein, in some measure help to raise the general standards of expression in even a minority of the performances throughout the country, the author will feel amply repaid for the time and effort spent in the compilation of this work.